Welcome, Jesus, to Our World

W. Brewster Willcox

HACKLEY PUBLIC LIBRARY
MUSKEGON, MICHIGAN

MAY 3 0 2013

Copyright © 2012 by W. Brewster Willcox.

ISBN:	Softcover	978-1-4797-1977-8
	Ebook	978-1-4797-1978-5

All rights reserved. No part of this book may be reproduced or transmitted in any form or by any means, electronic or mechanical, including photocopying, recording, or by any information storage and retrieval system, without permission in writing from the copyright owner.

This book was printed in the United States of America.

To order additional copies of this book, contact:
Xlibris Corporation
1-888-795-4274
www.Xlibris.com
Orders@Xlibris.com
112211

Contents

Introduction 9

Chapter 1	Who Is This Jesus That Everybody's Singing About?	 13
Chapter 2	How Did Jesus Die and Who Is To Blame?	 22
Chapter 3	What Did Jesus Know and When Did He Know It?	 26
Chapter 4	How Did Jesus' Miracles Actually Happen?	 33
Chapter 5	What Was the Transfiguration All About?	 38
Chapter 6	Does Jesus Have to Be as Difficult With Us as He Was With the People of His Day?	 45
Chapter 7	Is Jesus Alive Today?	 53
Chapter 8	In What Sense is Jesus God?	 58
Chapter 9	Whatever Happened to the Second Coming?	 66
Chapter 10	Does Jesus Have a Sense of Humor?	 74
Chapter 11	One Last Question: Why the God-Man?	 81

Epilogue 89

Appendix 92
Acknowledgements 97

To the Memory of my mother and father, Ruth and Edward Willcox, who both conveyed the strongest Christian commitment to life and work to their children and yet never backed away from a thorough-going modern perspective on their faith; and who frequently reminded me, "Don't forget to write!"

Welcome, Jesus, to *Our* World

Introduction

A few years ago Amy Grant ago recorded a poignant Christmas song, composed by Chris Rice, that has suggested the title of this book: "Welcome to Our World." She sings to Jesus a greeting fitting for his coming into our world today, a greeting that moves most Christians, when they hear it, to feelings of empathy and devotion.

Yet this song carries with it some of the ambivalence I feel about the sentimentality in much popular Christian piety of 21st century America. I wish in these pages to expose these mixed feelings, but I hope also to offer fairly a more mature and contemporary perspective of the Lord we Christians follow as our faith encounters a modern worldview informed by science and our more recent human history.

My journey to the perspective offered in this book began as a negative gut-reaction, but it has progressed lately to a more even-handed and thoughtful assessment of today's Jesus-language that we hear so regularly in so-called "praise-music" and in some public expressions of faith.

I admit that this bias of mine issues from both a secular rolled-eyes reaction to the insipid romanticism and narcissism of some Christian faith and from the intellectual critique of a seminary-trained Christian professional. I resist, however, letting either of these biases shape my final assessment. Instead, I'm trying to speak in a friendly, down-to-earth conversation with the thoughtful Christian layperson of today in, for the most part, a layperson's language. In those few instances where I do fall into more theological vocabulary, I hope I slow down a bit to define terms with humble apologies.

Returning to Amy Grant's song, I think all Christians respond in agreement with its petitions for Jesus' help, "bring your peace into our violence," and "heal us," and maybe even the thought that his blood "will save us." Yet what serves as the focus of this book is the notion that we have a world that we can offer to Jesus as our gift to him, as duplicitous and imperfect as it may be. "Make yourself at home," she sings. "Breathe our air and walk our sod," she sings. "Wrap our injured flesh around you."

It's this latter message of **welcome** that is closer to what I would like to convey in these pages. It is our place to offer now to Jesus whatever we know and experience in our time and our place to live. It is a troubled world, to be sure. Often in the forefront of our minds, it is the wars and terrorism and the struggle for domination and economic advantage against competitor nations and competitor corporations. Conflict and struggle is what we read about in our newspapers and that fire up our political campaigns and our nation's strategic planning. Yet there is more to it than that.

In modern times we do things in a big way. We have world wars and great depressions and global climate change. Nothing we do today is totally local: it always affects someone else, whether it's an exploited labor force or a colonized nation. Yet if you compare our world, especially our western or developed part of the world where you and I live most of our lives, to the world Jesus was born into, I think most of us would say we have a better world than Jesus knew. In our value system, if not entirely in reality, we have moved on from slavery and the divine right of kings and patriarchal oppression of women and children. We have found the cure of plagues, if not fully implemented it. We have democracies in the place of kings and caesars. We have food enough for everyone, if not the delivery systems and the political stability to make it available to all. The social issues that Jesus spoke about in his first century Galilee and the religious oppression that he ranted against in Jerusalem have largely become minor complaints that are dealt with through our American judicial system.

In short, the world we offer Jesus is a better world than he knew.

But more than that, it is a **different** world than his, a world of science and technology that he could not possibly have understood in the first century but which would certainly be a part of his hopes and influence in our day. To understand Jesus in our time we must necessarily translate him into our age, as diverse and as imperfect and incomplete as it may be for us. The aim is not to decide between liberal or conservative faith, but up-to-date, authentic faith. We need to think of Jesus here and now, informed and fortified differently than we read about him speaking to his friends and challengers in the first century; and then to imagine how in turn he would fit into our everyday experience and make his unique contribution to it. We must open the door of our world to him and invite him in.

So, welcome, Jesus, to *our* world. It's not at all the world you knew in Galilee; but it **is** our world, and it's the only world we can offer you. Make yourself at home here.

And, by the way, we have some questions, some uniquely modern questions, some questions your first-century friends failed to ask you, about how you now fit into our world today. We need your help to get down to these questions now.

I

Who *Is* This Jesus That Everybody's Singing About?

With more than fifty years as a parish pastor in the United Church of Christ (UCC) with two graduate divinity degrees I have been painfully aware that I am very much like the proverbial "jack of all trades and master of none." I am not a credentialed theologian. I am not a professional musician. I am not a historian. I am not even a rocket scientist or a particle physicist! But I have been convinced that I need to know something about all of these disciplines, plus a lot more, to carry out my calling. So I ask you, the reader, to bear with me here. We are all in a new time that we all are just learning about.

Theology informs a lot on what follows, music a little, and particle physics, you will be relieved to know, almost none. But they all—and you can imagine the "lot more"—come into making up a believing Christian in today's world.

Music has become in the modern church the primary medium for conveying the normative relationship with Jesus, who is, of course, the central figure of our faith. It hasn't always been that way. Jesus gave us sacraments to connect to him. The apostles gave us a story to tell, and preaching has given shape to the church's living faith from its very beginning. The ancient church produced creeds. Later we were given catechisms. Today we have prayer groups and bible study groups, and we still recite the creeds and distribute the bread and wine. But music has become the top billing for getting in tune with Jesus.

Of course, the church has always had its music to express and experience our communion with our Lord. From earliest times it has sung the psalms and composed "sacred songs," some which we recite to this day although the original music itself is lost. From plainsong to versified psalms the church's music has grown and matured toward the high mass and the chorale and eventually performance music. J. S. Bach transformed worship in the European church with fresh new chorales throughout the church year, while the eastern church was making an ethereal and thickly harmonic chant standard in its daily worship. Hymn writers proliferate in the church since the Renaissance, from Isaac Watts to Charles Wesley to Ralph Vaughan Williams. The English choral tradition is appreciated world-wide, and African-American spirituals and gospel music are sung universally today.

Through it all, of course, the eucharist and the catechism still persist as ever, to put us, in the words of St. Paul, "in Christ". Preaching had its hayday in 18th and 19th century America and well into the last century. During the same time the Sunday School movement was educating lay people, as many adults as children, and since World War II Bible and prayer groups were organized, grew and proliferate producing a church much more in tune intellectually with the historic Jesus.

But it is music which in the last century and a half has caught the heart of modern Christians and opens the most convincing channel to their faith and experience with a living Lord. A great variety of music styles and text circulate throughout the church. Hymn festivals and Christian rock festivals are frequent and elaborate. Congregations expect higher quality of performance in worship and support elaborate and expanding music ministries in local churches. If church musicians complain of poor salaries it is because they are being asked do more and do better without the commensurate compensation. Concert quality music in our churches today is expected, and that expectation is met with high dedication by both professional and volunteer musicians.

All of this development in the church is to be applauded, and you will not find any greater appreciation for the music produced in our churches than that which this author feels for the worship experience in his own church.

Yet there is a cost in these trends. It is the dissipation of thoughtful theological content in the music that has moved on and beyond the preaching in the 21st century church. And this lack of clear direction in our understanding of our faith and our communion with Jesus comes at a time of questioning and skepticism about the church's historic faith in the face of modern science and the contemporary world-view.

Our music in the church should support a more mature and modern perspective of our faith, but I find that it is letting slip away what could be a welcome recovery of the church's historic faith in a space age.

I admit my somewhat irrational aversion to much of the contemporary Christian songs that go by the enigmatic term of "praise music." The term prompts the question, Is not all music used in Christian worship praise music? What does the name say about itself and about the rest of the Church's heritage of hymnody, ancient or modern? Have we not been praising our creator-redeemer God in all our church music since the beginning of the Church's history?

Well, whatever! Let us accept, with some tongue-in-cheek, the usual nomenclature and move on to the issue at hand: my knee-jerk reaction to a popular and widely-utilized Christian music genre. It is this "Jesus-music," what a past music director at my church called "Seven-Eleven music": seven words sung eleven times until we finally move on. Yes, it's simple and joyful, and what Christian could object to music that is focused on our Lord and Savior, the center of all Christian worship? Well, the problem is what seems to be implied not so much by the words sung by the rock groups who now attract crowds to many of our sanctuaries but by the mood induced by the music.

"Jesus, Jesus, Jesus"—the name is repeated over and over and the singers appear to be in a swoon, as if the Messiah of God is some sort of rock star or movie idol. The music is simple and melodic. It elicits, not the jumping and swinging movement that we've come to know of straight-up rock 'n' roll music, but rather a slurry of sweetness that transforms the worshippers into a sea of swaying bodies and raised arms. As I take in the scene I am consumed with feelings of my own awkward embarrassment. Others seem to drift off from the reality of the moment into what seems like a trance imposed by the music's flow and volume augmented by powerful amplifiers. I am more conscious of my own conspicuous immobility than of what others are doing. What is wrong here? Is it the music? Is it I?

I believe it is neither the music nor your humble writer. What we have here is a failure of **theology**, a lack of vision of **who** this Jesus is that we are singing about. It is a serious failing because it is dividing our worship of him who forms and shapes our faith, and who indeed gives us a world-view that should shape our everyday activity in a world that has been visited by God and blessed for our rightful inhabiting of it. Where we belong as servants of this Christ is right where we are, in this 21st century and this space age. It's not a world that's easy to live in: it's challenging and hard to comprehend and risky. But it's where God has put us, and Jesus is the key to figuring it out and giving us the courage to keep at it. This is the Jesus we should be singing about, not a Jesus still back in first century, or even the 19th century, who had very different challenges and resources for meeting those challenges than what we do today. We need to worship and sing about a Jesus who lives in **our** world.

I look for excitement in the Jesus music of today, to prick some interest, but there is none. No surprises, no dissonances and key progressions, no inversions and extensions that I have come to recognize in jazz and classical music. Polyphony would be heresy. I am disappointed. My embarrassment disintegrates into boredom. What attracts people to this music? It must be the utter simplicity of it. It is music that seeks not to be music per se but only a mood-generator, by the large sound and lack of surprise.

The eroticism of much contemporary Christian music misses the mark: it's the **Spirit** of Jesus, not the flesh-and-blood Jesus, that we worship and that we should sing of in our Christ music. It is the Holy Spirit, the presence of the absent Jesus that our faith is focused on. Jesus sends us into our world with his Spirit, like a parent who sends a child from the safety and comfort of the home out into a world of wonder and challenge and—let every parent tremble in contemplation—a world of **risk**! And yet . . . . And yet the parent knows, or should know, that the child hopefully has internalized something of the parent, something of the spirit of the home, as one of many gifts with which to make one's way through life. Jesus promised his disciples that they will be better persons after he goes. Without him in the flesh and blood, "even greater things than I do will you do in my name because I go . . ."

To illustrate where I am going with these ideas, let me take four hymns from contemporary Christian worship, written in the 18th, 19th, and 20th centuries, which sing about Jesus in traditional but very up-to-date theological respectability. I have selected them from one worship service in the congregation where I now sit in the pew and not at the pulpit. The service is chosen totally at random (You'll have to trust me on this).

One hymn interestingly is explicitly a "praise hymn," in praise of Jesus nonetheless. Another is contemporary, written specifically for the Mennonite Hymnal, not a sort of radical liberalism to be sure. A third addresses the second person of the Trinity as "Word of God," not likely to run rampant with Jesus on the dusty roads of Galilee imagery but alluding nevertheless to obvious characteristics of Jesus' earthly ministry. And the last is written by the Unitarian poet-preacher, Harry Emerson Fosdick, for the dedication of Riverside Church in New York City. Only this last steers clear of any overt reference to Jesus Christ—not a surprise from the pen of a Unitarian!—but it is full of applications of "your ancient church's story" to 20th century urban and global ministries of the contemporary church.

There is much love of Jesus in music of contemporary Christian worship. "When morning gilds the skies . . . may Jesus Christ be praised"[1] How more explicit can it be than this! And yet it is Jesus the **Christ,** the anointed one, God's Messiah, now revealed through his death and resurrection, not seen as the friendly if enigmatic prophet of the Galilean hillsides. It is significant that St. Paul, writing in the early era of the Church not during Jesus flesh-and-blood lifetime, refers to this Lord always as "Jesus Christ" or "Christ Jesus." It is entirely to Jesus in this perspective that Paul wishes to speak. It is not to a familiar companion that it is comfortable to nuzzle up to and walk and chat with. And so with this anonymous German Catholic hymn-writer it is imagery of today's universal struggle and challenge, "discordant humankind in this your concord find," and "Be this the eternal song, through all the ages long, may Jesus Christ be praised."

"How Lovely Is Your Dwelling"[2] is a new hymn to me that I had not sung before that Sunday of February 13, 2011

---

[1] "When Morning Gilds the Skies" (1700's), translated by Edward Caswell (1854). The full text of this hymn and the others that follow in this discussion can be read in the Appendix.

[2] By Janice Janzen (1991).

when it showed up in my home church's worship service. My hymnal attests to its 20th century Anabaptist origin, from which one might expect some enthusiastic pietist ruminations about bosom love for or from Jesus. Yet what do we find here? It's a hymn that could almost have been written by the Unitarian Dr. Fosdick. It isn't Jesus language here but God language, God immanent, God active in God's world, God in three persons from a Mennonite point of view certainly, but not a flesh-and-blood Jesus who exudes human affections.

Next, my congregation and I sang about the "Word of God Incarnate!"[3] none other than the second person of the Trinity, the Word who "was made flesh and dwelt among us, full of grace and truth." This is the Jesus we encounter in the 21st century, who is as relevant now as when John wrote about him. This is the Jesus we should be praising today in our devout, heartfelt worship: "this treasure we have from you, its source divine, a light to all the ages throughout the earth doth shine." Of course, we love this Lord, but it is a love expressed less in ecstatic passion than in faithful struggle in the world, as the author of this hymn was noted for his work among the poor in London's East End.

And to close our worship on that occasion we sang that immensely popular paean to divine assistance in the human condition from Fosdick's pen[4], sung to the tune of this traditional Welsh hymn, 'Guide Me, O Thou Great Jehovah." A God of **grace** and a God of **glory** is praised for wisdom and courage in the "facing of this hour." Its melody recalls

---

[3] "O Word of God Incarnate," William W. How (1867)
[4] "God of Grace and God of Glory" (1930).

the passion of many Welsh male choruses whom we have heard singing those older verses of praise for God's guidance to a pilgrim in a barren land; but the Unitarianism of Fosdick focuses on, shall we say, the more heroic efforts of a **modern** pilgrim within a societal, and yes, a very urban and academic, milieu. Yet the 20th century hymn still references a God who comes to us in our human efforts to give our best and fullest to God's enterprise in this world. It is an acknowledgement of God's descent into our human world that makes this Unitarian hymn, as much as the others in my congregation's worship, a praise of the human Jesus, our companion in God's work.

Our Christian music, and specifically our hymns, must convey a challenge and an expansion of who we are in our everyday and modern context. It is not that simplicity, romanticism or sentimentality are always out of place in Christian music. There is always room there for that child-like softness that draws us into worship by pure feeling and ecstatic pleasure. But I only appeal to Christian worship planners to keep in mind and heart the Christ who comes to us to send us forth, and whose love for us fires us for leaving our comfort zone and for sharing that love in the world we live in today.

So now let us get to the work ahead to fill the void of a 21st century theological perspective. That is what this book is about. It seeks to find what Jesus uses from our world, an age brimming with new knowledge that has never been known before and new problems for us to tackle that have never been faced before. Jesus is the same Lord who came into our world centuries ago, but surely he has a new word to say to us today. As we say in the UCC, God is still speaking.

II

How Did Jesus Die and Who Is To Blame?

As a United Church of Christ minister for some 50 years, I've had thoughtful people and some impertinent confirmation students raise challenging questions with me around the season of Lent—questions that suggest how many people may wrestle with the implications of the Easter story.

I remember, for example, one gutsy confirmand who wondered, "How can you blame Judas or Pontius Pilate? Weren't they just playing roles assigned them in a drama that had to happen? Either they're blameless or they ought to be thanked for helping along a new faith."

My brother-in law, who is a far more accomplished writer than I and an insightful commentator on public life, is aware that not all bad behavior arises from a free will. "Weren't Christ's crucifixion and resurrection preordained? he asked me. Without them, there'd be no Christian faith, right? If Jesus had died in a back-alley mugging or of some wasting disease, the story of Christianity wouldn't be at all the same. In fact, there wouldn't be a story!"

Actually, these questions have bothered theologians and philosophers for ages. I guess you could say these skeptics are in good company, but they are somewhat missing the point.

How I answer these questions may not measure up with the orthodoxy of the church fathers of 2nd to 4th centuries, or even to some 20th century theologies. But many influences of the modern era—like the enlightenment, our outrage with anti-Semitism and various scientific and historical discoveries—push us Christians to take a fresh look at what the biblical record was really saying about the events leading up to the crucifixion and how Jesus' followers came to terms with the resulting crisis of faith.

Historically, I think the blame for the crucifixion pretty clearly falls on Pilate. He knew that Jesus and his movement were not dangerous. But there were many zealot rings in Jerusalem at the time who **were** violent, secretive and (most ominously) seditious. Pilate made an example of an available celebrity once the people had rejected the more obvious choice—Barabbus. While Jesus had been an embarrassment to the Jewish leaders, I don't think they really were bothered enough to execute him. Still, if Pilate wanted to take him on, they weren't going to stand in his way.

Making a blanket condemnation of the Jews is inappropriate. John's label of "Jews," who called for his crucifixion could just as easily be translated "Judeans," people of the southern country as opposed to the "Galileans" (who were Jews, too, of course) who had accompanied Jesus to Jerusalem.[5]

---

[5] Paula Fredriksen, of Boston University, has written the definitive study on why Jesus was crucified, in her book, *Jesus of Nazareth, King of the Jews*, Vintage Books (1999.)

Theologically, the claim that Jesus "died for our sins" doesn't come from the Gospel records. It's a later formulation based on criminal law of the time, and a substitutionary interpretation of the Old Testament sacrifices. The Passover lamb was not killed to take the blame for the nation's sin but to serve as a covenantal meal in which nation and God were reunited in their proper relationship of love, righteousness, and justice. Jesus in the Last Supper didn't claim that God was about to kill him to substitute for a punishment rightfully due us sinners. He said simply he was going to his death that "you may be one with me, as I and the Father are one."

While there's a pretty good consensus among the gospel writers about what happened at the crucifixion, there are all kinds of reported experiences with the resurrection.

Some saw only an empty tomb and drew conclusions. Others saw a phantom-like character who mysteriously appeared and disappeared through locked doors. Still others saw and touched a physical body, or an ordinary sort of human being, whom they later concluded must have been Jesus. In other words, the crucifixion is relatively objective, but the resurrection is very subjective, a different experience for whomever experienced it. And what do you do with Paul's "road to Damascus" experience when he heard a voice but saw nothing, and all of it years after the ascension when presumably Jesus would no longer be walking about on earth?!

So, what did the crucifixion-resurrection mean to the followers of Jesus who witnessed it? I think for them it was an awesome, life-changing realization that God has sealed a permanent, once-and-for-all reconciliation that they simply had to tell everyone about. Certainly, it can be that same life-changing event for us in the 21st century; but first we must see it for what it is. It is, and was, a massive miscarriage of justice that betrays the utter corruption of many human systems in this world. In that, the crucifixion of Jesus was not unique. What **is** unique about it is that a circle of perceptive followers of his saw it as a gift from a merciful God. They believed from that moment God was at large in their world in an invasion of God's Love, never to be daunted!

The moral responsibility for Jesus' death is not important if we pay attention to the real point, that God is making something good out of human perversity. It was a *Good* Friday, after all!

III

What Did Jesus Know and When Did He Know It?

Since the days of Watergate the definitive question to determine a person's innocence or culpability has been, What did somebody know and when did he know it? Knowing too much and knowing it before everybody knew it is not always a good place to be in. I never heard a church member put this question to me in quite this way about Jesus, but it is one that I have always had in the back of my mind when I try to interpret for my parishioners just what this enigmatic man means to us in our modern times.

Our Lord knew a lot of things and knew them well while he walked the dusty paths of this earth. Most Christians attribute to him a quality of moral innocence that is not found in the average human. And yet some 21st century moralists have attributed to Jesus extraordinary bits of knowledge that seem to put him in some questionable moral gray area, if not clearly in a position of possessing guilty knowledge. Why, for example, didn't Jesus say something in the way of condemning human slavery? Why did he have no compunction about the way wives and daughters were treated in that clearly patriarchal society of his time? Why didn't he have something to say, one way or another, about homosexuality and abortion and gambling? We in the 21st century would like to know what he thought about these common issues of our day.

We excuse people of that day who were not so morally sophisticated as we in this modern enlightened era think of ourselves, but Jesus was different, wasn't he? He stood above the crowd, and we might expect him, at least, to see a lot that was wrong in his day. He was God, after all, wasn't he? Well, yes, but he was also a man, and a creature of his own time.

As much as Christian dialectics have tossed around various theories of the divinity of Christ, orthodoxy has seldom wandered very far from a hard and fast view of Jesus' real humanity. Only rarely in the history of Christian doctrine have free thinkers dared to suggest that Jesus was anything other than human. Once in a while someone will suggest that Jesus was only an **apparent** human mortal. In those few instances that someone has tried the notion that Jesus was some sort of divine avatar or religious superman the idea has been quickly and summarily knocked down as rash heresy and faulty thinking.

The best known of the rare attempts to make of Jesus only the appearance of a human man is called Docetism (from the Greek "dokeo," to seem). It's the belief that Jesus' physical body in general and the crucifixion in particular were only illusions. This view of Jesus is that he was purely spiritual and not corporeal, and subject to ordinary human limitations. Docetic interpretations require making the passage metaphorical in John 1:14, "the Word was made flesh," and the motive for doing so seems to be to make Christian teachings more acceptable to pagan ways of thinking. But Docetism is considered heretical by most Christian theologians and was specifically condemned by the early Church fathers vociferously and in the orthodox creeds.

In modern times the concept is still considered deeply suspect in most church circles; but it has recovered some popular credence as Jesus is compared to modern super heroes and spiritual conjurers and magicians in the popular media and cultic radicalism (For example, "Jesus Christ Superstar")[6]. The appeal of the notion that Jesus was above common human limitations is somewhat whimsical, but it becomes more serious in popular ideas that Jesus knew or could control the future and effect natural events, or that he could cause people to become mesmerized and manipulated by his super human powers.

The New Testament record contains no such assumptions about Jesus, although the non-canonical so-called New Testament apocrypha often contain fantastical stories of Jesus' childhood and early adulthood where he performed vengeful acts of magic against people who challenged him or annoyed him. But the important conclusion to all these super-human notions about Jesus is that the church never makes any serious use of them in teaching the faith or in pursuing serious theological reflection on the meaning of Christ. There has never been any need to ascribe to Jesus more than extraordinary but thoroughly human knowledge and skills of a natural human

---

[6] My take from this popular Andrew Lloyd Webber musical is that the "superstar" status of Jesus was attributed to him by some of his followers but was not at all in Jesus' own self-understanding.

being of the first-century Middle East. Orthodoxy has never seen any reason to assume Jesus knew any secret or divinely communicated knowledge about the natural world or human society that would not have been achievable by any intelligent, observant and thoughtful human of his time and geographical location.

The New Testament, of course, does ascribe to Jesus amazing powers of healing and wonders that clearly were recognized by the people of his time as extraordinary. But it should be understood that the first century world was well populated with magicians and shamans who regularly performed wonders similar to what were observed by Jesus' efforts. Wonders were expected of any legitimate prophet or teacher in the first century world, and were not at all unique to Jesus. And it is even more to the point that Jesus himself was somewhat uneasy with the attention that his miracles aroused and even more dismayed with the public preoccupation with this aspect of his ministry. He did not himself focus upon his miracles but conceded to the people's struggles with disease and infirmity to show his compassion with human suffering.

The Gospel of John makes the miracles of Jesus the occasion for teachable moments concerning what is important about Jesus' ministry, namely his relationship to God and God's coming Realm. The Fourth Gospel amasses a collection of wonder stories that were current in the church's memory of Jesus and sets each of them as the occasion for a discourse on the nature of God revealed in Jesus' ministry. Each of the wonders is reported with due reverence and amazement from those who observe them; but then the narrative changes focus from the physical reality of the event to its spiritual and didactic implications. It is not what Jesus is **doing** but what God is **saying** in the ministry of Jesus which is important. Jesus is an ordinary man through whom God is making an extraordinary declaration!

What Jesus knew was what most competent human leaders knew in his day. He knew much about what we would call human psychology, but he knew it by having lived intensely and sensitively with his family and his people for the three decades of his life. He knew his Hebrew scriptures and the intricacies of the Jewish faith. And he knew something more, that we will explore further in a moment, about what was important in that religious tradition and what was worthy of less attention and reverence in the scriptures he knew.

What Jesus knew **nothing** about, however, includes a lot of what we take for granted today, ideas and assumptions that make up much of our world view and psyche, but are not irrelevant to his ministry today. He knew nothing of modern physics and cosmology. He did not think as a philosopher of the Scholastic period nor as a mathematician or scientist of the Renaissance nor as a social reformer of the modern era. We should not impute to him such understandings of the world and human beings that were unknown by anyone in his day and that further are not necessary to an appreciation of what he did know and focused on as important in his life and ministry.

The world as the historical Jesus conceived of it was a three-tiered universe of a Heaven above the earth and a Hell of isolation and punishment below. At best, he pictured the universe in the Genesis 1 framework, of dry land with waters above and below separated off by a heavenly Firmament.

He accepted as a given the patriarchal social structure of his birth. He accepted slavery and monarchial government and heterosexual marriage as normative in human society. He disapproved of many realities that he observed daily, such as political oppression of the poor, religious oppression of the less-than-morally-pure populace; but he never initiated any reform movements other than his well-documented "Way" of love and justice and reconciliation that the world has revered him for.

What Jesus **knew** in an emphatic and transformative way was that this world of struggle and conflict and oppression and, at best, of competitive victories and negotiated compromises—a world that we of the modern era would describe as a Darwinian survival of the fittest—was overlaid with a value system that is more real than the reality we have normally known, a value system characterized by love, compassion, justice and mercy. He saw life as two paradoxical worlds, both real, both created by God, both demanding human skill and dexterity to be successfully negotiated; but both also impacted by the other. And one of these worlds is true and the other is True with a capital T.

So where does this leave us in finding a way through to some of these most aggravating moral debates going on these days in the Christian Church? It leaves us with a job to do! But I find a lot of people are reluctant to get at it. Maybe it seems like it's too hard—it's easier just to take tradition as it's handed down to us. Or maybe they feel they shouldn't be instilling too much of themselves in saying what's on God's mind. But this is exactly what Jesus told us to do!

Jesus told his disciples that those who believe in him will do the works that he was doing. **And**, and get this! "even greater works than these will he do who believes in me, because I go to the Father." He said that of the likes of **us**! But he added that he would be sending a Helper, namely, the Holy Spirit in his place.

We are the ones who get the job from now on. Paul said, Don't despise prophecy, but test everything. No one knows our day and age like we do. We have prophets and teachers and the good sense that God has given us. We cannot read it from ancient texts and out-dated philosophies. **We** have the task of applying Jesus' Gospel to our own time. Jesus made it clear to us long ago, there's no one else to do it.

The early Church did it with dietary laws and rules of purification. The Renaissance Church did it by doing away with crusades and holy wars. The 18th century did it with divine right of kings. The 19th century Church did it with slavery. The 20th century, with the struggle for women's suffrage and child labor laws and civil rights. Now it's our time in the 21st century to decide what God says is right and wrong in regard to economic policy, birth control and abortion, homosexuality, and a host of other issues in our current culture wars. As we say in the UCC, God is **still** speaking. And the Church should be **listening** to what God is saying, and letting the world know what we've been hearing from the ebb and flow of the Holy Spirit.

IV

How Did Jesus' Miracles Actually Happen?

Let me begin this essay by admitting baldly I cannot possibly answer the question of the title. Thousands of philosophers, theologians, scientists and pseudo-intellectuals have attempted to attack this issue, and I certainly cannot add to their wisdom and foolishness! However, to my undying frustration, it is a question that never fails to be raised by a roomful of bright and challenging confirmands, not to mention some unnerving friends of mine who like to engage me in religious discussions, to see where the limits of my wisdom fail.

There is a glaring and irreducible disconnect between what modern science and just common sense knows and the biblical record of Jesus' wonders. Some of the healing miracles can possibly be explained by phenomena we have come to accept in the 21st century. We have learned to expect the human mind and body, when they're under stress or when extraordinary resources of self-healing are called upon, can come up with some fascinating solutions. People have been known to apparently die and lie in a coma for a spell before spontaneously coming "back to life." Certain sensory deficits have been restored under some stressful circumstances. And in a psycho-social context, when there's an obvious need for sharing, enough food might well "appear" from people's spontaneous generosity to feed a crowd of thousands. Not all wonders from Jesus' ministry are alien to our modern experience.

Such rationalizations have been suggested from time to time to help satisfy a modern scientific curiosity about events that occurred in a pre-scientific setting. However, I find them only minimally helpful myself, and no such imagining seems at all satisfying for dealing with the raising of a dead man four days in the tomb or a severed ear instantly reattached in place.

You don't need to "believe' the miracles in order to believe Christ, of course, especially inasmuch as Jesus himself made little of their importance for the nurture of faith. He spent far more of his time and energy playing down the effect of his wonders on the faith of the masses of people who were following him than appealing to these miracles as evidence of his authority. He tells the throng who are trying to tag along with him after the feeding of the five thousand, "Very truly, I tell you, you are looking for me, not because you saw signs, but because you ate your fill of the loaves." For him the causal relationship was the other way around: faith is what made his healings effective. They were not to prove his authenticity. And also for us in the 21st century the healings do not bring about a sincere faith. Rather, the negative impact that miracles stories have on the modern rational mind to understand our faith makes it necessary for us to get over the off-putting distance we feel about first century credulity so that we can focus on a more reliable foundation of our shared faith. The wonders are part of the story of Jesus, but not an all-important part, and certainly it is not in them where we come to know him best.

So, some sort of translation of the biblical narrative into a fathomable, if not totally believable, form is helpful to make the wonder stories consumable for the modern believer.

We can, at least, understand the points at which our conversation with people who first experienced Christian faith can become difficult. If we can at least acknowledge that parting of the ways and come to terms with it, perhaps our way to unity and understanding with the **faith** of the first century church will be more comfortable. We and they pay attention to very different details, but to the essentials of the Gospel we can be in complete accord.

We and they have the same instinctive understanding of how things happen: when "b" follows "a", then any sensible person would see that "a" **causes** "b," an easy explanation that seems to work out most of the time in life. We also are probably no more sophisticated than they are in pausing to reflect longer in those rare instances where "a" usually has not been seen linked together with "b" in the past. Usually it takes more than a simple utterance, like "Be clean," to initiate a healing of leprosy, but to someone who has never heard of an end to a leper's disease, any attempt at a cure might seem plausible and worth keeping an open mind about. But to those of us, who may never have seen a case of leprosy but are aware that it still exists in the world and great numbers of cases are cured routinely by antibiotics and bed rest, might be excused if we are a little skeptical when someone offers a miraculous short-cut.

We of the 21st century are not that different from first-century people in being confronted from time to time with events that leave us puzzled and without a satisfying explanation. Reports from particle physicists about their discoveries and their theories of reality at the sub-microscopic world where they do their work, pile on one inconceivable oddity after another and ask us to have faith that they know what they're talking about. Weirdness and eeriness are as much a part of our world of paradoxes as any age before us. The difference between us and people of a more primitive time is that we immediately assume there **is** a practical or scientific explanation, though we don't yet have it in mind. We immediately ask ourselves, "How did this happen?" The first-century, pre-scientific world "knows" instinctively what causes whatever is curious or wonderful, by simply looking to whatever immediately preceded it. They don't know **how** but they immediately know **what** causes miracles: somebody said something or did something immediately before it happened. They simply don't ask the sort of questions that we do.

Our 21st century minds have been taught to go back further and look deeper to some alternative sequence of events that might have made the causal link to what has attracted our curiosity. We have learned that nature sometimes plays a sleight-of-hand with us, and we want to ask the magician, "How did you do that?" Rarely, however, he does give up some of his secrets, enough times at least that we are bold to ask again the next time, and we have faith enough in the way the world ordinarily works to know that there probably **is** an answer to our question even if it's never been explained to us.

So, we are capable of going on without knowing, and that is perhaps the best we can ask for in the case of most of Jesus' miracles. Believe them or not is our choice, but don't let them get in the way of believing what precedes them, namely, Jesus' compassionate love, and eventually what follows, a faithful Church and bold Christian service.

V

What Was the Transfiguration All About?

Six days later, Jesus took with him Peter and James and John, and led them up a high mountain apart, by themselves. And he was transfigured before them, and his clothes became dazzling white, such as no one on earth could bleach them. And there appeared to them Elijah with Moses, who were talking with Jesus. Then Peter said to Jesus, "Rabbi, it is good for us to be here; let us make three dwellings, one for you, one for Moses, and one for Elijah." He did not know what to say, for they were terrified. Then a cloud overshadowed them, "This is my Son, the Beloved; listen to him!" Suddenly when they looked around, they saw no one with them any more, but only Jesus.[7]

This story of Jesus' Transfiguration has always intrigued me, and somehow I think it's central to the main theme of my

---

[7] Mark 9:2-8 (NRSV) =Matt. 17:1-8, Luke 9:28-26.

ministry, as I struggle to deal with the collision between the this-worldly human psyche and the sublime spiritual realities of Christ's impact on our world.

Aren't we just a little puzzled by this strange remark by Peter? Here these three disciples have just witnessed perhaps the most sublime moment of their lives in this shared spiritual envisioning of Jesus in the company of Moses and Elijah, and the best thing that Peter can come up with is some inane remark about how fortunate it is that the disciples are there, so they can build a shelter for everyone. When Luke narrates this same event, he feels he has to apologize for the senseless remark and explains that Peter didn't know what he was saying.

One commentator on this story of the Transfiguration describes Peter's impulsive remark as "half-related to the supposed situation, semi-reasonable, and yet fundamentally foolish." And he concludes,

> The remark by St. Peter is precisely the kind of remark . . . which might be made by [someone] in a dream, or in the strange, half-hypnotic condition in which [people] see visions [and hear voices].[8]

Perhaps that's the best that can be said about the remark, that it shows just how dazzled Peter was by what he had just witnessed. To try to make some sense out of the substance of the remark, or, worse yet, to try to allegorize some hidden meaning behind it, would be a waste of our time. It was just

---

[8] A. E. Rawlinson, *St. Mark* (London, 1925), p.118.

a thoughtless babbling that hardly deserves our remembrance of it, except for the fact that it occurred on the heels of the most holy event in Peter's whole career as a disciple, short of the crucifixion itself.

Peter must have wished many times he could have eaten those words or erased them forever from remembered history. But the ears of the other two disciples had heard the foolish remark, and from them it was recalled and repeated—and from that point on there was no squelching of the record. And when the event was told and retold, Peter must have often demurred with a smile, "I can't believe I said that. Did I really say that?"

Yes, Peter, you really did!

So what's the point of retelling just one more of the many times when Peter's impulsiveness left him with egg on his face? Well, one reason for telling it the way it happened is that it gives us a strong basis for believing that the story is reliable history. If anyone were to make up a story about such a mystical moment, they would never have put into it a senseless remark like that. Nothing that strange can get away as fiction—nobody would believe it! It must be true!

But another good reason for our remembering Peter's strange words is that they show us how stunned he was by the scene of Jesus and Moses and Elijah conversing together. What really could one possibly say about that? But, then, Peter, you know, always had to say something about everything—that's the kind of man he was! He was one of those people who can't stand to leave silence in its pure, pristine state, but has to clutter it up with the litter of his babbling mouth. He'd never heard of Abraham Lincoln's wise caution, "It's better to remain silent and be thought a fool, than to speak up and remove all doubt!"

Peter was a blatherer, but not a fool. More than once he desecrates the holy silence with his inane remarks. Jesus graciously ignores Peter's impetuous words on this occasion, but at other times he'll have to scold him, "Get thee behind me, Satan!" Good sense and reason were not Peter's strong points!

But there's yet another point for remembering Peter's strange remark, when we ask ourselves what it was that has so unsettled the impetuous Peter. It makes some sense in the context of what Jesus had just lead them through. What it is, is what it always is when he gets to babbling his foolishness. Matthew tells us that Jesus and Moses and Elijah were talking; and what they had been talking about was the fate that awaited Jesus, his death and resurrection.

Whenever Jesus starts talking about the suffering he is to suffer and the death he is to die, that's what always sets Peter off. "Don't talk like that, Master," Peter always says. "God forbid, Lord!" and "Though they all fall away because of you, I will never fall away," Peter protests. But Jesus has to say to him, "Get behind me, Satan" or "Truly, I say to you, this very night, before the cock crows, you will deny me three times."

Peter really has a problem when Jesus' ministry involves suffering and defeat. He simply doesn't want to hear about that. Deny it, protest it, change the subject—something! but don't ever let such negative thoughts come into the discussion.

That, after all, is why Peter has such a big mouth. It's because he can't stand what his ears are telling him. In this regard Peter is not unlike ourselves. We hate to hear negative thinking. Keep it upbeat, we say. We can't have any defeatist attitude, after all. But Jesus, the perennial realist, insists on looking at his fate straight in the eye.

Psychologists tell us about what they call, "psychic dissonance," when what our eyes and ears are telling us so totally contradicts what we want to hear that something has to give. Some people go berserk. Sometimes a person just has to run away. Sometimes a person commits suicide.

And sometimes a person has what we call a moment of truth, an "ah, ha!" experience—a spiritual awakening. These are moments when people frequently hear voices and see visions, when they report that the sky opened up or they were struck by blinding light, when they knew that God had spoken in their lives. These mystical experiences break through the psychic contradictions that refuse to be postponed or put aside any longer. When spiritual necessities press upon us relentlessly, usually the result is dramatic and life-changing!

And the Transfiguration of Christ was one such moment in the lives of Peter and James and John!

The world has often recounted stories of great conversions of heathen and lackluster Christians to the full convicting power of Christ's Gospel. There's St. Paul and St. Augustine. There's John Bunyan, the writer of *Pilgrim's Progress*, and John Newton, a former slave-trader who later wrote the favorite hymn, "Amazing Grace" to describe his conversion. There's Martin Luther and John Wesley, and the great Russian novelist, Count Leo Tolstoy, and the great American preacher, E. Stanley Jones. Each is a story of a radical turning of a life from aimlessness and sin to faith with great conviction and great energy! And the outward change is obvious for the whole world to see—we can't miss it.

But what about the inward change? What created it? What did it consist of, in the deeper soul of a person? Twentieth century psychology is beginning to let us see into the mind and soul of people. We can see better now the inner struggles with guilt and shame that force the spirit-altering experiences that create these great lives we revere from the past.

Eric Ericson has written a penetrating analysis of the psyche of Martin Luther in his prize-winning book, *Young Man Luther*. Ericson lets us see how Luther's struggle with his tyrant father on earth pushed him relentlessly into the futile attempt to satisfy a tyrannical Father in heaven, until one day in a flash of inspiration, Luther arrives at a humble faith in a merciful, heavenly Father, who justifies Luther by God's free grace alone. Luther's conversion wasn't in a psychological vacuum—it grew out of a struggle with his role as a son hopelessly trying to satisfy a overbearing father who could never give appreciation and approval to the young man.

So there are many influences in each of our lives, for good or ill, that create the context for our faith development; but, in the last analysis, it is we ourselves who each have to take our leap of faith. After we have wrestled in our souls with the devils that afflict each of us, and have considered the offerings of faith that Christian neighbors do lift up from time to time for our spiritual well-being, we find ourselves, as it were, on a precipice reaching out for an invisible hand of God. Will we grasp it or not? It is the question of our lives. It's a moment of irrational surrender, a madness that circumstances—or God, however we wish to describe it—thrusts upon us. And we can either descend into despair and escape—or slightly shift our weight into the unknown and discover that there is indeed another Power waiting there to receive our heavy lives in a new balance between heaven and earth.

That new state of spiritual balance each of us discovers for himself or herself; and the discovering itself is accompanied by a great variety of visions and blinding lights and crashes or still, small voices, each peculiar to the particular new child of faith born in that moment. But, varied and peculiar as these turning points of faith may be, there is a universal quality to all of them: it is a settling effect, a fitting together—as if the awkward and ill-fitting parts of a person's life have been given a shaking about and then permitted to settle back into a new and more meaningful, more functional, more faithful configuration. A raging earthly father was no longer the model for a heavenly Father who is merciful and gracious, but simply an accident of birth from which Martin Luther can escape. And doting, smothering mother-love was no longer a cosmic trap for Jonathan Edwards but simply a launching pad from which his prophetic ministry of radical evangelical faith could rise.

Every religious conversion is a release from some earthly burden which had become a demon, so that now faith can be more appropriately focused on a heavenly God who frees us by the simple fact that God cannot be grasped and packaged in the earthly garb of all our failing false-gods.

VI

Does Jesus Have to Be as Difficult With Us as He Was With the People of His Day?

I used to have a lot of misgivings about some of the passages in the Gospels where Jesus is talking to people who come to him with only a partial understanding of his message, trying—at least it seems to me—to get a better handle on him. I think I might have been worried that Jesus might be dealing with **me** in the same way. Does Jesus really have to come down so hard on the rich young ruler who asks what he has to do to enter the Kingdom of Heaven? Sell all you have, give it to the poor, and come follow me. Isn't that a little extravagant?

Or the Syrio-Phoenician woman, that is, a non-Jewish woman, who has heard a little bit about him and thinks he might be of benefit to her in her struggle over her ailing daughter (the Bible says she had a demon)? He tells her, Sorry, I've come only to the people of God's covenant in the scriptures. Her time hasn't come yet. Fortunately, for her—and to Jesus' public image among modern-day ecumenicists—she's a woman with a little moxie who isn't going to be sent away so easily. He's told her, You can't give food to dogs! that is meant for the children. (Oh, Jesus, did you have to say that?) But, saving the day, she comes back at him: "Even the dogs can eat what crumbs fall from the table."

What an insulting position she has put herself in—if, anyway, everybody in this story is being totally serious, which I suspect they are not! In both of these stories I think we are seeing Jesus' sense of humor showing through. And we shall have to take a closer look at Jesus' use of humor in the next to last chapter of this book, because I am convinced that Jesus' humor, which the people of the first century could understand much more easily than we can, is part and parcel of Jesus' message to the world of his day and to us.

But for now, however, let us simply acknowledge that Jesus could be rather difficult with the people who ventured forth to enter into conversation with him. We know well he could be extremely critical of the Pharisees, who were the super-religious lay people of first-century Israel. Some of them clearly had no intention of pursuing an open, give-and-take dialogue with Jesus. They were more intent on tripping him up. So we probably figure they had it coming to them.

In either case, with friendly and unfriendly inquiries, Jesus could be pretty confrontational by the standards of our polite society today. So we wonder, does Jesus have to be that difficult with **us**?!

Jesus had confrontations with lots of people. Not all of them were really his enemies. Even the Pharisees, the usual bad guys in many dialogues, didn't have any serious disagreement with him. They were just aghast at how lackadaisical he could be about some of the purity regulations that seemed so important in their religious life. They were always asking him, How can you let your disciples be so negligent about these accepted practices of our tradition? After all, Jesus was operating as a rabbi, and the Pharisees were part of this rabbinical system and only trying to follow it in strict adherence. They were more scandalized than being defensive by Jesus' relaxed attitude about ritually required washing and what constituted work on the Sabbath. They thought they had the right take on these disciplines for themselves, and they just wanted Jesus to get with it.

Jesus could also have his little tiffs with the oily sycophants who from time to time would come to him with flattery and servile requests for confirmation of their high opinion of themselves. That is, after all, what was Jesus' problem with the rich young man who only asked what he needed to do to be saved. We can imagine Jesus rolling his eyes! The young man, we're told, went away sadly, or "gravely" (NRSV), because he didn't get the answer he wanted. How much more satisfied the man would have been had he had the gumption of that Syrio-Phoencian woman to stand up to Jesus and continue the conversation. Zacchaeus, in a similar position vis-à-vis Jesus, after all, came away from **his** encounter with Jesus with a much happier outcome.

But it wasn't the flatterers, or even the Pharisees—who were, after all, just trying to do their best in the rabbinical scheme of thing—who got the full vent of Jesus' wrath. It was the religious authorities who began to see that Jesus represented a real threat to their professional standing and well-being. It was the scholars and priests who showed the most anger toward Jesus and eventually began to plot to do away with him. (Of course, as a religious professional myself with two divinity degrees, I do get uneasy about these conversations of his with priests and scribes—more on that later!) Jesus' issue with the Pharisees was their moral and ritualistic separatism from the normal run of humanity. His advice to them was, Just let up on these friends of mine who are not offending God and pay attention to the real priorities of the law which requires Israel to adhere to a society of inclusion, justice and love toward neighbor.

With the Pharisees Jesus' attitude was mostly, Just don't get me started! He quickly points out the essence of the problem and sends them away muttering. The most rage he expresses toward them is with their observance of the Corban law, which wasn't so much a creation of these lay people themselves but a gift to them from the religious lawyers. It allowed them a legalistic sham to confiscate property from one's parents, technically as a sacrifice to the Temple but often ending up in the hands of a selfish son, in obvious violation of the commandment to honor one's father and mother. The real culprits, of course, were the lawyers and the agents of the religious domination system emanating from the Temple in Jerusalem.

Where Jesus really shows signs of "breaking loose" is when he begins to deal with this larger system, "this evil generation," in his words. It's where Israel's religious underpinnings have come apart, with the merchants profiteering within the walls of the Temple, with the fraudulent use of the Corban Law, with so much attention focused on the minutiae of the law when the whole religious system was corrupt. No sign, says Jesus, will be given for this evil generation other than the sign of Jonah, which had set a precedent for a complete regeneration of the entirely corrupt city of Ninevah.

So, yes, Jesus could be a pretty difficult person in his dealings with many people he encountered in the course of his ministry. The question is, Would he come across as angry with us in the 21st century and our religious and political systems today? Of course, he might. There is plenty of corruption, plenty of domination systems, plenty of religious practices that serve more to manipulate and separate people from each other than to unite them as a people of God. The important thing for us to ask ourselves is on which side of these issues do we find ourselves. To be sure, Jesus might be extremely angry with us. But let us also notice that, while Jesus could be stern at times with his own disciples (to Simon Peter, for example, "Get behind me, Satan!" when he stood in the way of Jesus' taking his own mission to Jerusalem), he stayed with them and never displayed with them the kind of rage he reserved for the perpetrators of an evil generation. Let us be confident that Jesus could be mercifully compassionate with a lot of our lesser foibles. We shouldn't get so caught up in minor church squabbles and family bickering, to forget that there is always a way back to Jesus and his compassionate eyes.

Nevertheless, we also need to remember that we can find ourselves sometimes complicit with the many ways today in which people are exploited in business, politics, and international affairs. These do rouse Jesus to peaks of anger today, to be sure, that are comparable to what we read about in the Gospels. And I have to face the fact that the Church to which I have responsibility to lead could well be the focus of Jesus' anger. Once it was a church that gave aid and support to the divine right of kings and sanctioned slavery and the subjection of women in the home and government. We have moved on from those issues, but today we know of clergy who prey upon innocents, with sexual abuse of children and financial manipulation of congregants, of intrusion into sexual privacy of marriages and exclusion of gays from the institution of marriage and prevention of divorce from marriages that fail.

All of these injustices against common people have been perpetrated by religious authorities of today. Without a doubt Jesus is offended by these outrages, He called down injustices of his day such as the Corban law and harsh punishments for moral offenses and commercialization of the Temple. Religious people are never exempt certainly from Jesus' anger, but that was in first century Israel. Today my ministry to which God calls me is to serve others, not to judge them or ostracize them or to regulate their lives. To preach Christ today is not to convert persons who follow other beliefs or who have no belief, but rather to earn their respect and perhaps by that effort provide gentle influence to their lives.

Now we have come upon the real challenge of Jesus to our modern responses to his first century declaration, "The kingdom of heaven is at hand! Repent and believe the good news." as Jesus did, picking up John's well-spoken message for his own ministry after John was arrested. It is an all-inclusive commitment he asks for, but it is also clearly a call to setting our priorities right.

We shouldn't be afraid of Jesus' harshness: it is good news, after all. A friend of mind tells me of the experience of a preacher he knows who admitted to a glowery attitude one morning as he drove below a dark drizzly sky that well reflected his mood as he groused to his wife beside him. She, however, told him to turn around (the literal meaning of the word for "Repent") and see a different view. When he turned around—well, actually he looked in the rear-view mirror—what he saw was a beautiful sunrise. A whole new outlook on life!

Jesus' harshness is his compassion. Liberals and moderns are in dismay over "fire and brimstone" preaching of a different age, but its motive was good news. We might have a different list of evils today. To the sins of alcohol and prostitution we might add smoking, drugs and gluttony today, maybe spouse abuse and greed. Certainly racism and homophobia and anti-semitism. But if it is preaching that is moved by Jesus' "Repent," it is delivered with compassion and a desire for a new outlook for our world.

And, finally, what characterizes Jesus "difficult" attitude at times is his uncanny skill to cut to the chase, to the priorities of God's realm. And there in that context what is most important is the unity of the people of God. There should be no one-up-manship, no exploitation, no exclusivism, that separates humanity from humanity. All those whom Jesus gives a hard time, including us in the 21st century, he ultimately receives with justice and love.

Jesus clearly saw himself in the role of the Old Testament prophets and would couch his ministry in their words:

> . . . and what does the Lord requires of you but to do justice, and to love kindness, and to walk humbly with your God?[9]

and

> . . . let justice roll down like waters, and righteousness like an everflowing stream.[10]

When we get edgy about how feisty he can be with some people in the Gospels it's time to take a hard look at ourselves and make the necessary adjustments.

---

[9] Micah 6:8.
[10] Amos 5:24.

VII

Is Jesus Alive Today?

I shouldn't even have to touch this question. It's the very basis of Christian faith for ninety-nine percent of any Christians who have ever lived. St. Paul says it as plainly as it can be said: "If Christ was not raised, there is nothing in our message."[11] This challenge is definitely directed at me as author here: if I can't handle this question, the whole effort of this book is useless. So yes, Jesus is alive today.

But the evidence for this central truth of Christian faith is not to be found in the fodder of which this book seeks to feed on. It comes from realities and commitments completely prior to any thoughts entertained on the pages of our discussions here, and cannot be doubted without making this whole effort vain and hopeless.

None of the questions of this book would be asked—with any urgency, at least—by anyone who has not first seen the truth of Jesus' continuing life in the on-going ministry of his Church. As the textbook of my seminary course in biblical theology states it:

---

[11] I Cor. 15:14.

> The principal argument for the truth of Christ's resurrection does not consist in a skilful piecing together of the documentary evidence of the Gospels, or even of the NT as a whole, but in what the Church does every Sunday in the quality of her life on every day of the week. When the church meets to break the bread in accordance with her Lord's command, she not only proclaims his death (I Cor. 11:26), but also witnesses to his resurrection. The weekly celebration of the death of a dead leader would be no occasion of joy and thanksgiving, and the fact that from the earliest days the disciples met to make joyful memorial of his death, re-enacting the solemn scene in the upper room on the night on which he was betrayed, is the strongest possible evidence of the certainty of their knowledge of his resurrection.[12]

No, the question for us here is not whether or not Jesus is alive today, but **how** he is alive for us in the modern understanding of how things happen in our everyday world. Yet even allowing for our radically different perspective on nearly everything compared to the world-view of people in biblical times, we need to ask ourselves, what is unchanged about our perceptions of Jesus from those of the early church?

In the fourth chapter above we made an attempt to understand the miracles in light of what we have learned about how things happen in our day. This, of course, presented little problem to the people in Jesus' day who would never have to

---

[12] A. Richardson, *An Introduction to the Theology of the New Testament* (1958), p.190.

ask the sorts of questions we do today. In that earlier discussion we had to leave the question pretty much as an unanswerable one. Some simply incredible reports of wonders, that might teach us some worthy lessons in the power of faith and some insight into the mind and heart of Jesus at the moment, had to be left unsolved. But we can take some consolation knowing that Jesus himself did not wish to convey the notion that his wonders were a secure foundation for faith in his ministry.

In other words, we can be content to leave the question of how his miracles were possible as a side issue in the effort to appreciate his reality in our 21st century. Not so, however, about his resurrection. Now here we have come upon a real crisis of faith.

How shall we live with this Jesus who enters our modern world to be with us? How shall we pray to him? How shall we listen to him? How shall we see him indeed present with us in the context of activities that are of crucial importance to us but which are totally out of the picture whenever he comments on the common human events of his day. What can we ask of him about terrorism, about medical care and psychological therapy, about homosexuality and test tube babies, about our loneliness as one life-bearing planet in a universe of rocks and fire? If Jesus is alive for us today it is not as social philosopher or meditation guru. He is something other. What is the impact he has on our modern lives today?

It is clear that Jesus, although he was, after his death, a life-changing presence for the people who knew him in the flesh and blood and was, in their minds, the same Jesus they had known before, was not the same kind of living Jesus as before. The risen Christ is always coming and going. He "appears" to them in a locked room and then is gone. He is face-to-face with Mary just outside the tomb and walking with two disciples along the road to Emmaus, but they don't recognize him even though they had seen him only days before, until he addresses Mary and breaks bread with the disciples. People who knew him well encounter him again but they are told not to touch him "because"—enigmatically—"I have not yet ascended to the Father." At one time he consumes a fish, at another passes through a locked door. Every encounter is different and loaded with questions and mystery. What is this life that he now shares with the disciples? What is the life he continues to share with them, and with us, after the ascension?

No one in the Gospel records asks the kinds of questions we might ask in such curious circumstances—where has he gone between appearances? and what **about** his "ascending"? Unlike the people of his day, we've **been** there, at least vicariously with our astronauts, and believe me, there's nothing there but rocks and fire and a little bit of human debris. Heaven for us is no longer a place but an attitude, a perspective that God is around us like a protective Firmament. It's hard for us to think of Jesus now as a physical entity or of his going and coming as vectors in spacetime. Instead, we speak of him as a "spiritual" life, but meaning what?

The spiritual reality is not a different reality but the same reality looked at differently. Let's say that again. Spiritual reality is not a different reality but the same reality looked at differently. The shepherd isn't just a shepherd but the Good Shepherd. The water he gives is not just water but Living Water. The bread he gives is the Bread of Life. The spiritual life Jesus offers us is in the real, ordinary world but seen differently.

As we will see in a later chapter, Jesus' divinity is not at all like the God we thought we knew but as the Messiah who will suffer and die. As God's Israel went through an Exodus, and God's remnant through an exile, we are God's redeemed world having passed through the Cross with Jesus and carrying that sign with us now in this world. This is the Life that Jesus still bears in our 21st century.

In this we are no different from the disciples and the early church. The only fact that is important is that he is alive while he had been dead. What's important is what was important in his being with the disciples before the crucifixion, namely, the truth that "God so loves the world"; and the promise "Peace I leave with you, **my** peace, not the world's peace"; and the response that should be elicited by his living again among us, namely, "Have this mind among yourselves which you have in Christ Jesus, who . . . ."[13] You should know the rest.

Jesus is alive today, and that makes everything different.

---

[13] Phi. 2:5-11.

VIII

In What Sense is Jesus God?

This question takes us way beyond the scope of this book and probably also way beyond the intellectual capabilities of your author. In the deepest sense this is not an issue in biblical interpretation but one in theological construction that deserves a review of centuries of church deliberations.

Certainly, we will not go there in this essay. Nevertheless, there is a hint of an issue here in the record of Jesus' life and ministry, even before the re-workings of the memory by the early church that we discover in the Book of Acts and the letters of Paul and other authors at the "back" of the New Testament. I refer in general to Jesus' own self-understanding so far as we can get to it through the early theological re-shaping of the story of his ministry, and specifically to what are called Jesus' eschatological Son of Man sayings.

Now, just a word of apology to the reader for the appearance of this theological term when I have promised earlier to keep things simple in these pages and a word of explanation to clear things up a bit. "Eschatology" is simply the area of theological and biblical studies having to do with "last things," that is, the end of world, or the end of an evil age, the final judgment, and in relation to the meaning of Christ, his "Second Coming." From all four of the Gospels there is a packet of sayings from Jesus that are loaded with images of an exalted and triumphant Son of Man who introduces this final period of history. Moreover, it is quite clear that Jesus means them in reference to himself.

Beyond this aside, I also must admit some hesitancy to even getting into this question, because there is no way that I can avoid offending many readers, both liberal and conservative. But this is a question that is always coming up to me in classes I teach about Jesus and informal discussions in a variety of contexts in our day. Still, I feel I have something to say to the curiosity and some confusion on the part of many thoughtful Christians today, at least at the level in which we can discuss Jesus own understanding of his role in God's saving initiative in the world.

I must let the reader understand that I am a child of the modern liberal church (Congregational/ United Church of Christ) and a product of a liberal college and seminary education (Oberlin and Yale Divinity). Yet I begin this ambitious task of searching out Jesus' divine nature with the assertion of the English theologian of the New Testament, Alan Richardson, who wrote in the middle of the 20th century what I believe still stands in our 21st century:

> When once we have shaken off the liberal presuppositions which have dominated so much New Testament research from Harnack to Bultmann, we recognize that the assumption that Jesus himself thought through (humanly speaking) the problem of his own

existence and taught the answer to his disciples make far better sense of the historical evidence than all the attempts of the liberal critics to explain the evidence away.[14]

In the early part of the 20th century a great many studies of the "historical Jesus" were attempted by a host of scholars trying to get at what is reliable history behind all the theological interpretation built into the gospel record. This era came to a screeching end with Albert Schweitzer's *The Quest for the Historical Jesus* (1911), in which he argued it will be forever impossible to reach a reliable consensus about what really happened and what was really said about the life and ministry of Jesus because of an essential over-riding eschatological bias among all his chroniclers. Schweitzer thereafter quit his theological studies, pursued a medical degree, and spent the rest of his life serving as a medical missionary (and a notable organist) in Lambarene, The Congo. In the post-World War II period a group of English biblical theologians, including such divines as Alan Richardson, Thomas W. Manson, C. H. Dodd, and C. K. Barrett, took up Schweitzer's challenge by declaring, "Yes, we can discover the real Jesus by accepting that the troublesome Son-of-Man statements are authentic and therefore must be an essential dimension of any contemporary understanding of Jesus." The liberal German theologian, Rudolf Bultmann, considered these sayings as authentic but that Jesus was not referring to himself as the eschatological Son of Man but some other never disclosed agent of God. I

---

[14] A. Richardson, *An Introduction to the Theology of the New Testament* (1958), p. 125.

believe Bultmann was wrong in denying Jesus was talking about himself.

So what do these passages[15] tell us about Jesus self-understanding?

What we know of Jesus' own thinking about his relationship to God and his role in God's plan of salvation is derived from a complicated development of Jewish religious concepts that were common at the time and Jesus' unique reworking and combining of them. These concepts are that of "messiah," or "Christ," in the Greek language, and that of "Son of Man."

The difference is fairly well understood by Christians raised in modern Sunday Schools and with biblical preaching, between the Old Testament Jewish expectation for a messiah who would come and re-establish the old Davidian monarchy and the New Testament Christ who had no such political overtones. Of course, biblical scholars wrestle with many subtle nuances in Jesus' problem to fit in somehow with the popular messianic expectation in his day; but most Christians, I think, get the general picture here.

Where many modern Christians fail to appreciate Jesus' understanding of his own role in God's intervention in human history is in the heavily eschatological "baggage," when he referred to himself as "the Son of Man." At the base of it, this phrase in the Old Testament meant simply a real mortal human being, in the context of one or another divine interventions in Jewish history, as in the eighth Psalm, "what is man that you

---

[15] The complete listing: Mark *:38; 9:9; 13:26; 14:62; Matt. 12:40=Luke 11:30; Matt. 24:27;=Luke 17:24; Matt. 24:37=Luke 17:26; Matt. 24:44=Luke 12:40; Matt. 10:23; 13:41; 19:28; 24:39; 25:31; Luke 17:22, 30; 18:8. The editorial comments of Matt. 16:28; 24:30 and Luke 12:8 are also sometimes included.

are mindful of him, or the son of man that you visit him?"[16] God addresses Ezekiel (2:1) and emphasizes the prophet's mortality in contrast to the divine Presence: "Son of man, stand on your feet, and I will speak to you!" Or again, Daniel's vision (7:13) describing a clearly divine event but in which apparently a mere mortal is the principle actor: "I saw one like a human being (literally, "a son of man") coming with the clouds of heaven." Jesus almost exclusively uses this title for himself in contrast to the political implication of "Son of David," and the supernatural "Son of God" used from time to time by others addressing him. None of this from Jesus' mouth implies anything more than mere mortal status for himself.

All this being said, however, we still have this collection of exalted Son of Man sayings that clearly come loaded with triumphalist meanings which suggest that Jesus did have divine pre-conceptions regarding his role in God's salvation work. "... He ordered them to tell no one until after the Son of man had risen from the dead," and "Those who are ashamed of me and of my words in this adulterous and sinful generation, of them the Son of Man will also be ashamed when he comes in the glory of his Father with the holy angels," are among the more egregious utterances that sound extremely alien to our 21st century ears.

What can we say of a positive nature about Jesus' self-understanding and his eschatological expectation of "returning in glory" in view of our modern perspective of waiting twenty centuries for the fulfillment of this hope? We

---

[16] Rendered by the NRSV, being faithful to this fully human meaning but avoiding the archaic non-inclusive language: "What are human beings that you are mindful of them, mortals that you care for them?"

will look in the next chapter at how the early church dealt with the "delay" in his coming; but we have to wonder right here what can these sayings have for our benefit, living as we do in the 21st century?

We can say, first of all, there is nothing in any of the Gospel records that bestows on Jesus anything of the normally considered attributes of God, like omniscience, omnipresence, omnipotence. Jesus is seen clearly as a real man. His powers to perform wonders did not require him **being** God, of being anything more than a mere mortal. The closest we get to truly divine qualities in Jesus nature is the "Logos" passages in the prologue to the Gospel of John, but this divine title of Jesus is not referred to again in the rest of the Gospel and is not characterized as part of Jesus own understanding of himself. John's list of "I am" statements by Jesus—I am the Good Shepherd, I am the Living Water, etc.—characterize Jesus' **role** as clearly beyond the natural order of life, yet they fail to require his nature to be divine. The only explicitly Trinitarian reference in the four gospels[17] is widely accepted as a later addition to the record and not an authentic utterance by Jesus himself.

Yet still we have here these (from our modern perspective) troublesome authentic sayings from the lips of Jesus. If we are to bring Jesus into our century we have to bring him as he really was and with the near unanimous testimony of the church down through the ages that he was indeed divine **in some sense**. What do we make of him today?

---

[17] Matt. 28:19.

The answer to our question in this chapter is to be found in what Jesus himself believed made him divine. It cannot be found in the supposed superhuman characteristics of God which are never attributed to him in the Gospel record, for example, all the "omni's" that we noted above. When Jesus used the self-description of Son of Man, he is "a Messiah who suffers according to the Scriptures." The difference between the Jewish and the Christian conceptions of Messiah is that the Christ must suffer and it was this characteristic that the "Son of Man" terminology was to convey. So when Jesus replies to the high priest's question whether or not he is the Messiah (Mark 14:61-2), he is saying, in effect, "Yes, I am the Messiah, as you will realize when you see the Son of Man sitting at the right hand of power, and coming with the clouds of heaven"; or possibly, "Call me 'Messiah,' if you like, though I don't think it's very suitable; you will see who I am when you see the Son of Man . . . etc."

Thus Alan Richardson concludes his study of the "reinterpreted Messiah:

> A radical re-interpretation of [then] current Jewish notions about the Messiah is involved in the Son-of-Man conception in the Gospels, and it was made necessary by the deep spiritual insight expressed in the phrase 'the Son of Man must suffer.' It can hardly be doubted that the scriptural basis of this insight was Isa. 53 and the recognition that the suffering Servant of the Lord there depicted is a prophecy of the Messiah. . . . A brilliant new synthesis of OT themes had been effected, not merely

as a new theological teaching, but as the programme of action for the ministry of Jesus.[18]

We are led, therefore, to believe that the divinity of Jesus is derived not by his miracles and wonders, which, of course, in the ancient world would not have been seen as really very unique, nor in any radical new teaching from the Jewish law and prophets, which was derived directly from his scriptures; but rather in a bold teaching about a Messiah who would suffer and die. This is what is unique about Jesus. It is what led the early church to conclude that he was "divine."[19]

As Paul claimed, "We proclaim Jesus Christ . . . , and him crucified."[20]

---

[18] Op. cit., p,135.
[19] Op. cit., p.136.
[20] I. Cor. 1:23 and 2:2.

IX

Whatever Happened to the Second Coming?

This is not a new question. It's not even exclusively a modern question. Christians have been wondering about this since late in the New Testament era.

In almost every age of the Christian era anxious, perhaps one would say, impatient believers have felt the urgency of the immanent return of Jesus to usher in a new age of justice and vindicated faith. The cartoonish depiction of adventists of various ilk waiting of some hillside for the clouds to open on some appointed date is rare and extreme. The picture is indeed comedic except for the reality of lives needlessly upset and hopeful souls dispirited by the continuous failure of prophecy to produce the promised meeting. One wonders why people insist on setting a date when Jesus himself warned that the end of the age would come without any foreknowledge, lest his followers be lead astray by rash and manipulative apocalypticists.

The hope for the Second Coming of Jesus, however, most often in Christian history has not required the rush to some hillside but is expressed in a more thoughtful and responsible reflection in the real world that continues on for the time being. Modern-day Seventh Day Adventists and Jehovah's Witness certainly are respected for their seriousness for living within an unredeemed world, even if some of us find their frequent door-bell-ringing and street-corner evangelism at times annoying. These and other contemporary adventist groups show that looking ahead to the Lord's return is not at all inconsistent with social ministries and academic sophistication. And their example may suggest some deeper meaning in futurist thinking for more mainline Christians as well, as I hope we shall see in a moment.

But first, let us pause to defuse some rising impatience with some long words that I've already chosen to indulge in, and with fair warning a few further on to be encountered later. I apologize for having let the word "apocalypticists" escape undefined a couple paragraphs back, but the reader has no doubt become familiar with "apocalypse" in the popular media and may be aware that the final book of the Bible is sometimes referred to as "The Apocalypse of John." At any rate, it should present no problem if we keep in mind the more frequently used title of that writing: the "The **Revelation** of John." "Apocalypse" is simply the Greek word for "revelation" or "disclosure"; but it's usually used in reference to a class of writings that come out of Judaism and Christianity that focus primarily on expectations of divine intervention to vindicate the faith currently under persecution. Apocalypticists take these and other predictions of a future divine action as central to the expression of their faith.

Perhaps a little more obscure is a word we will have occasion to use in a moment: "eschatology." As I have noted above it refers to beliefs about last things, at the end of time, at death, or at a moment of judgment. There is no other English word or phrase which quite carries its meaning. "Life after death" is much too narrow a focus and "the end of time" is too philosophical or scientific with no appreciation for the effect of eschatology on our perception of the present world. Indeed, critical to our understanding of Jesus' second coming is an eschatology that is at once "realized" and "future."

A century ago a British theologian, C. H. Dodd, introduced to the world the concept of a "realized eschatology" arising out of the pages of the New Testament. In mid-20th century another Englishman. C. K. Barrett, expressed the discovery this way:

> ... the future tenses normal to eschatological speech are constrained to become present tenses in order to make clear that the end of history is in fact being experienced in the midst of its course.[21]

That is, **now** as history is still going on we already feel the influence of the end. The futuristic eschatology doesn't disappear from the New Testament because the "end" remains a true end, and history hasn't yet been brought to a conclusion with the appearance of Jesus.

---

[21] C. K. Barrett, *The Gospel According to St John*, SPCK, London (1955), p.56.

The paradox of both future and realized eschatology is expressed most clearly in the Gospel of John where the phase occurs twice, "The hour is coming and now is . . ." (4:23 and 5:25). The author wrote "from two standpoints." One explanation is, of course, that we read what Jesus said in the course of his ministry when the significant event was future, but we also see it in terms of the resurrection and Pentecost from which the Christian Church developed and is now a present fact.

But the paradox of future and present tenses is more subtle and more powerful than this! John was not satisfied with a sort of Jesus-mysticism, in which the worshipper was immediately united with him in a supernatural way, a simplistic romance cut away from real history, i. e., the so-called Andy-theology: "And he walks with me, and he talks with me, and he tells me I am his own." Nor was John happy with a simple apocalyptic eschatology of Jesus descending from the clouds and wrapping everything up in a neat heavenly construction. As Barrett goes on:

> The eschatological element in the fourth gospel is not accidental; it is fundamental.[22]

To have abandoned it would have been to abandon the whole framework of biblical Christianity, and run the risk of a purely metaphysical Christianity divorced from history. The dangers of mysticism

---

[22] Op. cit., p. 58.

"... are held in check by the constraint of the primitive Christian eschatology, which is a constant reminder that the Church lives by faith, not by sight, and that it is saved in hope."[23]

A commitment to live in this real world with all of its stress and struggle is easily read in the lines in the Fourth Gospel. It doesn't take a biblical scholar to detect a rising anxiety in the early Christian church in the late first century when the Gospel of John was constructed of memories and traditions of the Hellenistic church centered around Antioch. Three concerns were troubling Christians. The **passing of all the eye-witnesses** of Jesus' ministry and crucifixion, persecutions developing from **rising opposition** from Jews and from the Greco-Roman pagan religious power structure, and the question of **whatever happened to Jesus' promised return** to usher in some sort of end to the difficult conditions Christians were living under in AD100 Asia Minor.[24]

In the Gospel of John, Jesus is remembered challenging his followers to anticipate new truth from God by expanding their expectations about their own abilities and by being willing to take some risks. Christians aren't simply to wait for God's fulfillment of his promises. They are also supposed to participate in that fulfillment. They're not simply readers of revelation, they're also to be its instruments!

---

[23] Ibid.

[24] For a fuller discussion of the consequences of this historical context of John, see the author's unpublished STM (1971) thesis, *Gospel and Strategy,* residing in the Yale University Divinity School library. He apologizes for the blatant non-inclusive language of the paper, which was current at time of its composition.

This, I think, is an interesting new perspective on the freedom and latitude for future development in the Church. And it happens to turn up in the Gospel of John because of a unique view of history and future-time which the writer of John could appreciate around the year 100, that Paul could not yet see when he wrote his letters to the Thessalonians around the year 50.

When **Paul** was active in his missionary work in the middle of the first century, the Church enjoyed the strong charismatic presence of the apostles and their vivid personal recollections of Jesus himself. Paul also had a relatively short-range view of the future, expecting the return of Jesus and the end of the age at almost any moment. A developing, changing Church didn't really have too much meaning for him at that time (although his outlook changed considerably before his death about the year 70). There was no time for changing strategies. It was simply a matter of getting as many converts as possible into the fold before the end came.

But by the time the Gospel of John came along at the end of the century, the Church had a very different future to contend with. By now, the Church was feeling some anxiety over the passing of the apostles and the loss of their leadership. By now, all Christians were beginning to look ahead to a longer-range, more open, future. And most importantly for us nineteen centuries later than when this thought was beginning to sink in, the Church began to see itself less and less as a tiny Jewish sect, and more and more as a new world religion.

Now, it's interesting to see **what** the writer of John remembered about Jesus to help the Church along in these new circumstances. It was remembered, for example, that

Jesus had promised to "return," as the other three earlier gospels also recorded. It was also remembered that Jesus had promised to send, in his absence, "another Comforter," as he said, the Holy Spirit. Now, the new insight—let's say, the new **revelation**—to the writer of John was that these were essentially the same promise. The Holy Spirit **was** the presence of the absent Jesus, whose evidence could be seen all around in the courage and miraculous success of the young Church. What was going on was really the presence of Jesus in their very midst.

That meant that Jesus, through his Spirit, was always "returning," just as he had promised. He was always going before us, one step ahead of us, drawing the Church onward into God's promised future. So, in regard to God's interaction with the world, the Church wasn't just to sit there and watch it happen in front of them—they were becoming a part of it themselves! Moreover, the revelation of God wasn't simply something "back there" to be remembered and revered—it was also something "out there" to aspire to, and to discover!

In John's Gospel, the Jesus who says, "I am in the Father and the Father in me," is also he who immediately goes on to say, "he who believes in me will also do the works that I do, and greater works than these will he do, because I go to the Father" (14:10-12). Now, **that's** hard to believe, that Jesus was saying that about the likes of **us**. But that's what he said: "greater works than these" from people like you and me who believe in him.

What happened to the Second Coming? one asks. What happened is that it is happening now as we speak . . . and live . . . and tackle the greater works that Jesus calls us to accomplish.

In conclusion, let me simply tell a little-told episode of our American history as related by a great lover of America, the British commentator, Alistair Cooke:[25]

> The time was the 19th of May, 1780. The place was Hartford, Connecticut. The day has gone down in New England history as a terrible foretaste of Judgment Day. For at noon the skies turned from blue to gray and by midafternoon had blackened over so densely that, in that religious age, men fell on their knees and begged a final blessing before the end came. The Connecticut House of Representatives was in session. And as some men fell down and others clamored for an immediate adjournment, the Speaker of the House, one Colonel Davenport, came to his feet. He silenced them and said these words: The Day of Judgment is either approaching or it is not. If it is not, there is no cause for adjournment. If it is, I choose to be found doing my duty. I wish, therefore, that candles may be brought."

---

[25] Alistair Cooke, *One Man's America*, cited by John Mason Brown in *Saturday Review*, June 28, 1952.

X

Does Jesus Have a Sense of Humor?

My father-in-law, as a young man, left his home in Alabama and traveled north during the Depression to find a better livelihood, and probably offer some help for his family saving them from poverty. He lived a long and reasonably prosperous life in Lancaster, Pennsylvania—he died at age 98—, and he never left his traditional Methodist upbringing. Sometimes he liked to probe my more liberal take on matters biblical once in a while. One time he asked me, "Why didn't Jesus have a better sense of humor?"

My reply was a shocked disbelief, "My goodness! Of course, he had a great sense of humor! What about the parables? What about the camel going through the eye of a needle? What are you talking about?!"

What I might have said, but decorum held my tongue was: Jesus had a sense of humor: just not **your** sense of humor. His sense of humor was asking if you can find a man pictured on the back of a five-dollar bill. After you've wasted a few minutes looking and looking without success, he'd take the bill from you and look himself. "Oh," he'd say, "He must have taken the bus!" Roars of laughter would follow.

Well, that wasn't Jesus' kind of humor. Nor mine. But it was a step up, I suppose from the Methodist Sunday School of his youth.

Jesus' humor was typical of first-century Middle East. It consisted of large portions of hyperbole and, with his rabbinical style, his famous creative parables. He wasn't above a pun or two at times. "You are Peter, and on this rock (Greek: *petros*) I will build my church . . . ." But most of all, his style fell into a dry sense of irony.

A biblical scholar from Iceland, Jakob Jonsso, now deceased, introducing an article on humor in the Bible, begins with **ironic comedy**.

> Irony is a mode of expression in which what is said is the opposite of what is meant; consequently, ironic statements cannot be understood without rejecting their apparent sense. Humor starts with the perception of irony or of some other inconsistency strong enough to provoke confusion or tension. Sudden release from such tension often results in a smile or in laughter; the inner feeling is of sympathetic joy or playfulness.[26]

Jesus' exchange with the persistent Syro-Phoenician woman, recounted above in Chapter 6, is a perfect example of Jesus' playfulness. Any other reading of his original rejection of her request is unnecessarily harsh. Jesus recognized that he

---

[26] *Oxford Companion to the Bible* (1993), Bruce M. Metzger and Michael D. Coogan, eds., p.324.

had come upon a woman whom he could count on to counter his challenge one-for-one, and he wasn't disappointed!

Jesus could use humor and irony even in the most serious matters. He tells about comical people, a man who needed help in the middle of the night and refused to be turned away until he had roused a family from bed; a dishonest steward who was about to be fired and who makes friends for himself when he soon would be needing some friends, by cheating his master on their behalf; and a woman who knew she was up against a judge who had no sympathy for her poor status in the social order: she annoys him persistently until in frustration he gives up and grants her plaint. Who cannot see the humor behind these tales? That they are parables about being persistent in prayer does not diminish their comedy.

Irony is more than just a rhetorical technique, however. Jesus could use it to demonstrate the nature of his ministry. Some people get the joke, and some don't. "Let those who have ears to hear, hear," implying that those who don't probably will never understand!

In the Fourth Gospel which displays considerable further theological development from the synoptic gospels and as a consequence the appearance of more serious sermons to preach, is nevertheless a gospel structured on one lasting bit of irony. In John "everything happens simultaneously within two frames of reference."[27] One is the world of everyday occurrences, where people meet at a well for a drink or one observes a flock of sheep obediently following the familiar voice of their shepherd. The other is the life "born from above,"

---

[27] Op. cit., p. 325.

the world as seen from the perspective of the Logos, which is sublime, heavenly, eternal life. The incarnate Jesus and the eternal Christ are one and the same person. And everything he says and everything he does has a double meaning. And the result is a sort of irony, "two tunes interwoven into one musical composition."[28] And even the followers of Jesus sometimes do not catch the irony of Jesus' presence in their world, such as when Jesus is washing the feet of his disciples, he says "You do not know now what I am doing, but later you will understand." Then Peter objects that Jesus shouldn't be washing his feet, and again Jesus must explain the irony, "Unless I wash you, you have no share in me." (13:7-8)

Obviously, those who are locked into the everyday shape of things cannot begin to understand the sublime truths that Jesus is introducing to the world. On the other hand, those who only listen to the eternal side of Jesus' message have missed an important ingredient in the mix and will miss the humor and the zest of a beautiful human world. The earthy and the heavenly have to be taken together in one paradoxical whole to appreciate Jesus' recipe for eternal life.

As we welcome Jesus into our modern world we must not miss the irony with which he still comes to us. We should not worry so much about what we will eat or wear that we miss the holy food and raiment that we can consume in God's present kingdom. We should not be building larger barns to contain our material goods that overshadow eternal blessings. Both must be consumed together if we are to catch the drift of Jesus' double meaning.

---

[28] Ibid.

I have written and performed a monologue of Joseph the father of Jesus based on words and ideas in two previous musings about Joseph.[29] In it I express Joseph's disappointment that God has "distracted" him from the normal life he had always hoped for to be the married householder and artisan in his Jewish village, but acknowledges that "my wife had prior claims on her and my son wasn't my son." Instead, he lived his life in exile. In this tragi-comedic situation, what could he do? he asks himself.

> But in exile, what are your choices? One is, to escape, to defy the orders, to repudiate the claims on you, if they demean and humiliate you. Another is to surrender, give in, **accept** the claims on you, as though they are, after all, your destiny.
>
> Or, there is a **third** way: You may think I am going to suggest something halfway between escape and surrender. But there **is** no halfway. These are the only genuine responses, to fight or to join. The third way, I think, is to do **both,** simultaneously: renounce **and** surrender. Play your role heartily, as though it **were** the real thing, and disdain it with a hearty laugh, knowing it isn't. **You** may be playing a role right now, thoroughly playing it out, but you are not the role. You may own it, but it doesn't have to own you. Accept the script, but know you are more than any script. Live out the looseness and freedom

---

[29] W. B. Willcox, *The Power of Paradox* (2012), "Joseph's Surrender," p.73ff. It includes quotations from James Dittes, *The Male Predicament* (1985) and William H. Willimon, "Righteous Joseph: Embarrassed Among Men," *Christian Century,* Nov. 23,. 1988.

of hearty commitment with a humble sense of humor. That's what I ask you to try.

This "hearty commitment with a humble sense of humor" is, I believe, what Jesus asks of us in our modern lives. We are regularly making choices of career and for marriage and children, of stewardship of our time and private finances for family and church and charities, of medical choices and end of life decisions for ourselves and loved ones, and a host of other serious issues of both spiritual and worldly concerns. One may even entertain the notion of leaving a six-figure career in finance or law in favor of a sense of call to ministry as a pastor or missionary.

Finally, Joseph sees both the humor and the seriousness of his new destiny.

> You see, I didn't just tolerate these distractions, I lived vigorously into them. Like other "wise men" who, steadfastly and far from home, followed **their** distraction, a wayward star—like them, I gave my all to these unexpected, unwelcome intrusions into my plans, as if distractions conveyed meaning and destiny.
>
> And in the end they did! They intruded. They upset me. They turned my life around. They put me in touch with a **new** destiny, **And I claimed it!**
>
> And let me tell you something: the father who is not the father, **is** the father nevertheless! That surrender of the dream, that giving up of intimacy, that lifetime of ambiguous love, that's what it is to be a father.

> Fatherhood, like Godhood, is, after all, a giving of life, a giving in, a giving over, a **surrender.** You give your child a life to lead . . . and then you **follow**. No birthing for fathers, no weaning, no gradual transition to letting go.
>
> To be Joseph, to be a father, to be a **man**, is to give your all to your creation—all your energy, all your manhood, all your powers—put everything to work to make the creation a success. And then, when it is time . . . , to give still more . . . , by **surrendering** and letting go.

Finally, it occurs to me that the Jewish historic sense of living in exile is the sort of irony that I'm talking about, as it is played out in Bock-Harnack-Stein musical comedy "Fiddler on the Roof," It's based on the tales of Tevye by Sholem Aleichem. Tevye is annoyed of the "fiddler on his roof" who seems to be needling him in his poverty, and as he is losing control of his world of tradition the fiddler is driving him crazy. The play begins with Tevye's household preparing for the Sabbath, and he sings of "Tradition!" to hold on to his precarious life in Czarist Russia of 1905. But even Tevye can see the humor of his sad condition as he sings, ironically, "If I Were a Rich Man!" He senses the tragedy of time passing, as his daughters grow up and grow away from him. He sings of them and of his world that he loves but regrets its passing, in "Sunrise, Sunset."

Yet he triumphs when he gets the joke and laughs at the irony of his existence; and he celebrates his humble, fleeting life, "Lechaim!" To Life!

XI

One Last Question: Why the God-Man?

Ten questions we have discussed, a nice round number. Seems like a time to stop. But there is one more that begs to be considered, if we modern, clear-thinking Christians are to be comfortable within our faith in this world. It's a different sort of question than the ones we've been discussing. They have all been questions about the relevance of the historical Jesus in a modern-day world. But the question we are turning to here has certainly been implied in every one we've looked at so far.

The answer to this eleventh question is what makes of some relevance all the other questions that we ever ask about this man Jesus of Nazareth whom we now call Christ. It's the question of why Jesus at all? Why have so many people looked to this mortal human being as somehow crucial to their own knowledge of and contact with the Ground of their being? This is more than the question of Jesus' divinity that we looked at in the eighth chapter. It's not just, Is Jesus divine? or in what sense is Jesus divine? It's, **Why** is Jesus divine to **me**? Why is my relationship to God dependent on what he said and did?

For centuries, since the age of Scholasticism, Christian thinkers have been wrestling with the problem of squaring our faith with God by proving God's existence. It's not how many of us today come at the problem of faith, but back then it seemed useful for the dissemination of the faith to be able to demonstrate that God actually exists before one gets further into the study of what this God does and wants. In the 13th century Thomas Aquinas most notably took a hand in the problem and offered his famous five proofs for the existence of God.

All his "proofs" boil down to the same line of reasoning: Everybody sees in our world imperfect wonders that seem to imply a Perfection behind the good we encounter in creation, natural wonders, moral good, human reasoning, etc. If there's something "pretty good" in our world, something **perfectly** good must have put it there. Aquinas himself was an Aristotelian, but it helps to live in an intellectual matrix where Platonic essences are believed to exist behind every accidental. In a modern realist age, however, it's hard for us to see Aquinas' proofs as anything more than circular reasoning.

A century and a half before Aquinas, Archbishop Anselm of Canterbury had sparked the Church's interest with his "ontological" proof of the existence of God. Anselm began by defining God as that "than which there is no greater." Then he reasons, either God exists or God does not exist. If God does not exist, this cannot be the case because it's possible to conceive of something greater than God, namely a god that does exist; but this is excluded by definition. Therefore, it's **impossible** that God does **not** exist.[30]

This may not help us with our modern faith any more than Aquinas' proofs. If your head isn't spinning yet from this tricky reasoning, you may be ready for a suggestion of mine as to why this ontological proof fails. (Or you may not care a whit, one way or another, but here goes.)

The proof makes the slight-of-hand substitution of "existence" for "greatness." You would still have to prove that actual being makes a concept "greater" than non-being. If that is provable, then we might begin by defining God as "than which there is nothing 'real-er,' i.e., more real." But if you start off by **defining** God as the most "real" concept there could be, then you've pretty much stolen the match before it begins. Nevertheless, modern theological thought has found some value in the concept by defining God as "Being itself" rather than **a** being (Paul Tillich, followed by John Shelby Spong and many others). The implication of this is that God is outside of creation, i.e., not a being but instead the Ground of all being.

Now, don't feel too poorly toward Anselm. His later book, *Cur Deus Homo* (Why the God-Man) makes exactly the case I am trying to make here and a bit more elegantly that I'm doing right now. Anselm answers the question of his interlocutor, Boso, Why couldn't God simply declare that human beings are saved the same way that God created the world by simply saying the word and it was so? Anselm's answer in a great

---

[30] *St. Anselm: Proslogium; Monologium; An Appendix in Behalf of the Fool by Gaunilon; Cur Deus Homo,* Tr., Sidney Norton Deane (1903), Chapter III, pp. 8-9.

many examples is that, for the sake of God's love, one cannot expect humans to obey and love God by being compelled to. Love and righteousness presuppose human freedom and the juxtaposition of both the human and divine has to be present in any solution to the problem of human sin. You cannot bypass the paradox of the "God-man," nor can you expect to find the venue of God's redemption anywhere but within the sufferings and vicissitudes of this world.[31] The triumph of God's work of salvation is in the heart of human beings imbued with free will and human love. No other conclusion to God's efforts in this world of sin is suitable to be considered.

The first and great commandment is this: that you love God with your whole heart and strength and mind. And a second is like it: that you love your neighbor as yourself. No other command is greater than these: they comprise the whole law and the prophets.[32]

Putting this ancient summary of the answer to what God does and what God asks of us into the language of the 21st century, we might say we are faced with two great paradoxes of our faith. One paradox is that the great and mighty God of the universe, the Judge of human sin and the determiner of our fate has crossed this great chasm between us and God.

---

[31] Op. cit., pp. 177ff, especially Chapters VI to IX, pp. 185-197. But modern theologians would add to Anselm's "God-man" the stipulation that the human side of Jesus is truly and fully human, including not only his mortality but also the human limitations of his placement in time and social milieu. Whatever Jesus' divine qualities, he did not understand nuclear physics nor question the institution of slavery and patriarchal society nor speak in Elizabethan English.

[32] Comprising Mt. 22:36-40, Mk 12-28-34 and Luke 10:25-28. See also Romans 13:8-16 and James 2:8 that the early Church considered no greater good beyond full, complete, freely offered human love of God and neighbor.

But the other paradox, which is just as unfathomable, is that God has made us free to make our own faithful response to God and that we do in fact **sometimes** do that!

And this is the point at which Jesus, the God-man, the eternal Christ and the man of Nazareth, enters our lives and makes something wholly new of them. Jesus offers a solution that every religion of the world wrestles with: what to do with God? Just on the face of it, it is an ominous problem. Here I am confronted by Someone or Something that has complete control over me and against which I, a mere mortal, cannot have the least impact.

Religion is the human attempt to deal with this existential dilemma: I need God but God is beyond my control. In the early 20th century a little known German divinity school professor smashed onto the theological scene that had been psychologizing, secularizing, scientifically analyzing the study of world religions with a bombshell of intellectual and spiritual insight that has turned the course of inter-religious understanding and dialogue. His name was Rudolph Otto of Marburg University which had one of the most famous Protestant seminaries in the world, and the name of his book was *The Idea of the Holy*.[33] He defined the concept of the holy as "numinous," (from the Greek "*numen*," an unknowable reality underlying all things). Otto described the "holy" as a "non-rational, non-sensory experience or feeling whose primary and immediate object is **outside the self**."

---

[33] Rudolph Otto, *The Idea of the Holy*, (1917), published as *Das Heilige: Uber das Irrationale in der Idee des Gottlichen und sein Verhatlnis zum Rationalen* (The Holy: On the Irrational in the Idea of the Divine and its Relation to the Rational). It has never gone out of print and is available in about 20 languages.

(Emphasis added.) It is both **terrifying and fascinating,** at the same time. Many theologians, Christian and Jewish, have acknowledged Otto's influence on their own work, such as the American theologian, Paul Tillich and the popular British religion writer, C. S. Lewis.

It is this paradoxical nature of God that religion seeks to respond to. One writer, with somewhat tongue-in-cheek, described holiness as an electrical dynamo, the power of which we desire to appropriate but terrifyingly dangerous nevertheless if one gets too close to it. "The fear of the Lord is the beginning of wisdom!" We see what Otto refers to as the "mysterium tremendum" in the story of the Hebrew people asking Moses to cover his face after he had conversed with God on Mount Horeb, because "the face of Moses shone"; or again, of transporting the ark to David's new capital city of Jerusalem, recorded in II Samuel 6:1-11, when a servant Uzzah put out his hand to catch the ark when the oxen carrying it stumbled, and immediately was struck dead. Whereupon David had second thoughts about bringing such a dangerous object into his city. Centuries later the curtain in the Temple in Jerusalem separating the Holy of Holies from the secular world outside was less to protect it from desecration from an unclean world than to protect the world from too close encounter with the holiness within. St. Paul once described the Old Testament Law ("Torah") as a protective barrier for the Jew from the full radiance of God's blinding presence (II Corinthians 3:14).

Now, of course, much of both the Old and New Testaments conveys a faith that counteracts this fearful reticence before the face of God, but that this potential terror always lies behind the holiness of God cannot be ignored. And it is to this **softening** of holiness by all religion that I would direct our attention.

The mythologies of Greek and Roman and Scandinavian religions make holiness more amenable by denigrating the character of the divine to human-like motivations that could be coaxed and manipulated by clever or heroic mortals. Hinduism's softening is found in its ethical faith depicted in the Bhagavad-gita (The Lord's Song), where God is personified and depicted as a friendly director of ethical living. Taoism, the religion of the Chinese poets, teaches that the universe is directed by an impersonal "Tao" (Way) in which humans must learn to "go with the flow," when evil or misfortune confound our lives until "the way" eventually turns. Islam, which is usually seen in its unalterable witness to the infinite power of God ("God is great") when God's will is executed, nevertheless exudes as softer, friendlier faith in its mystic Sufi expression.

In the Hebrew religion that Christians share with our Jewish neighbors we know of the suffering Job who thrust an angry fist at an all-powerful God and complained, "How can you treat me this way?" to which God replies, in effect, "Who are you to question me? You are but a bug, an ant that I can crush beneath my heel if I bothered to pay you heed!" And yet, ironically, there Job is, still standing at the end of the story, his life restored to even grander prosperity and well-being.

From all these religions we get a glimpse of God's true attitude toward us mortals. God is not a hopeless tyrant. God is Someone or Something that you can actually respond to, even talk to and come away from, if not unscathed, at least wiser and with a more hopeful future ahead of you.

And in the case of the Christian "God-man" we can, because God gives us such freedom, sin! We can betray him, deny him, crucify him. Still God returns to us. All the world's religions offer some sense of God's "friendliness"; but when you really face the reality of the encounter with God, this is unbelievable! It's the impossible possibility, a God who refuses our very rejection of God! A Love that will not let us go.

God **is** Love. God's essence, as we see God in the God-man, is Love. It is not God's power, not God's all-seeing eye, not God's unchallengible Justice, that is the final word. All of these "omni's" are true about God, of course; but they are not the last word. God is all that God is by the way of Love. The dominant character of God is Love. Nothing else transcends God's Love. It is the final word about God.

The God-man and the Cross he bears confirm that. Jesus, the man of Nazareth, the risen and eternal Christ, conveys the indefatigable truth to us: Emanuel, God is with us.

Now let us welcome Jesus into our lives here and now.

Epilogue

This book has been structured with questions one might ask about Jesus. Now in this final word with my readers I repeat a question Jesus once asked of his friends.

Jesus did not often ask questions. Aside from several accusatory questions he put to his enemies—Pharisees, priests, and Pilate—, and a very few light-hearted proddings of his friends—the woman taken in adultery, some disciples and his mother—, I find only one question (in John, my favorite gospel) which he seriously challenges those who essentially believe in him but are revealing some hesitancy (as do we all at times, I'm sure).

As several of the disciples were fishing after the bewildering events of Good Friday, the risen Christ appeared on the shore. Not recognizing him at first, the men were probably slightly annoyed when he chided them with the question that all unsuccessful fishermen hate: "Children,.." (Children!! Indeed! Who's calling us "Children"?! Anyway!), "Children, have you any fish?" Well, No, not really. But he tells them where they may find some. A minor miracle, I suppose. But enough of one to make the fishermen forget the earlier indignity.

Anyway, moving on, when they had filled their nets—you know the story—they enjoy a happy reunion and a picnic breakfast around a warm fire.

Then it is that Jesus pops the real question. The question of their lives, really. The question they will never forget. The question that puts all their questioning and hesitancy in perspective, and is the beginning of a total disruption of their lives and a new destiny that will drive them to the end of their lives.

To Simon Peter, the spokesperson and representative of all of them, Jesus says:

Simon, son of John, do you love me?

Jesus, once he has survived the shock of entering our 21st century world, certainly asks the same question of us.

Do you love me?

Appendix

Here are the words of the four hymns discussed in Chapter One[34].

When Morning Gilds the Skies

Anon., Transl. Edward Caswall, 1854, alt.   Tune: Laudes Domini, J. Barnby, 1868

When morning gilds the skies, my heart awaking cries,
    may Jesus Christ be praised!
Alike at work and prayer, one purpose I declare:
    may Jesus Christ be praised!

New strength comes night or day when from the heart we say,
    may Jesus Christ be praised!
Let sin and evil fear, when this sweet chant they hear:
    may Jesus Christ be praised!

Discordant humankind, in this your concord find,
    may Jesus Christ be praised!
Let all the earth around ring joyous with the sound:
    may Jesus Christ be praised!

Be this, while life is mine, my canticle divine,
    may Jesus Christ be praised!
Be this the eternal song, through all the ages long:
    may Jesus Christ be praised!

---

[34] From *The New Century Hymnal,* Pilgrim Press, 1995.

How Lovely Is Your Dwelling

Jean Wiebe Janzen, 1991 Tune: Es ist ein' ros' or Psalm 84

How lovely is your dwelling, O God, my hope and strength,
> My spirit longs for shelter, my flesh cries out for home,
where even swallows nesting beside your altar resting
> are ever praising you.

How blessed are those whose travels are strengthened by your hand,
> Who pass through shadowed valleys and find refreshing springs.
Your rains fall soft as kindness on all your faithful pilgrims
> until they come to you.

Look on me, God of goodness, you are my sun and shield.
> One day within your household is what I most desire.
O guide me in your mercy along my lonely pathway;
> O bring me safely home.

O Word of God Incarnate

William W. How, 1867, alt. Tune: Munich, Harm. Felix Mendelssohn, 1847

O Word of God incarnate, O Wisdom from on high,,
    O Truth unchanged, unchanging, O Light of clouded sky:
We praise you for the radiance that from the hallowed page,
    a lantern to our footsteps, shines on from age to age.

O God, we hold this treasure from you, its source divine,
    a light that to all ages thought the earth will shine;
It is the chart and compass that all life's voyage through,
    'mid mists and rocks and tempest, still guides, O God, to you.

O make your church, dear Savior, a lamp of purest gold,
    to hear before all people your true light as of old!
O teach your wandering pilgrims by this their path to trace,
    till, doubt and striving ended, they meet you face to face.

God of Grace and God of Glory

Harry Emerson Fosdick, 1930, alt.   Tune: Cwm Rhonda, J. Hughes, c. 1907

God of grace and God of glory, on your people pour your power;
> crown your ancient church's story; bring its bud to glorious flower.

Grant us wisdom, grant us courage, for the facing of this hour.

From the evils that surround us and assail the Savior's ways,
> From the fears that long have bound us—free our hearts for
> > faith and praise.

Grant us wisdom, grant us courage, for the living of these days.

Cure your children's warring madness; bend our pride to your control.
> Shame our reckless, selfish gladness, rich in things and poor in soul.

Grant us wisdom, grant us courage, make our broken spirits whole.

Set our feet on lofty places; gird our lives that they may be
> armored with all Christ-like graces, in the fight to set us free.

Grant us wisdom, grant us courage, in the quest for liberty.

Save us from weak resignation to the evils we deplore;
> let the search for your salvation be our glory evermore.

Grant us wisdom, grant us courage, serving you whom we adore.

Acknowledgements

I attribute my peculiar perspective on the Christian scriptures to my seminary training and later graduate work at Yale University, and my readings in Karl Barth, the great German-Swiss theologian of the 20th century. I have attempted to communicate that point of view in all my years of Christian preaching and again in the pages of this book.

Beyond that academic history, I want to acknowledge a lingering dependence on the writings of what I call Britain's "divine gang of four," who saved Christendom from the Bultmannian "sell-out" in the post-WWII era, as I describe in Chapter 8 of this book. These four British biblical theologians were Alan Richardson (1905-1975), an Anglican divine who taught at Nottingham University and was Dean of York the last ten years of his life; Thomas Manson (1893-1958), an English Presbyterian, who taught at Manchester University; C. H. Dodd (1884-1973), an English Congregationalist at Cambridge; and C. K. Barrett (1917-2011), a Methodist at Durban University.[35] I read a great deal from all four during my

---

[35] A fifth name might be added to this list, E. C. Hoskyns, an Anglican priest of a similar mind with the other four, but I have not read any of his original writings, but am deeply in his debt for his translation of much of Karl Barth's *Church*

seminary days and in graduate school (both at Yale), and feel very indebted to their interpretation of the biblical tradition for a modern age. In the course of writing this book I found myself going back again to them (after many years of not really thinking much about them), especially Richardson, for clarification of my own position. They represented a middle ground between, on the one hand, what later would be labeled "progressive Christianity" but in mid-20th century was in academia referred to as simply "old liberal" ; and, on the other hand, traditional Anglo-Catholic teaching. I place myself today between the modern progressive Christian movement and the Roman Catholic and fundamentalist protestant expressions of the Christian faith.

Many persons have read all or portions of these pages before publication, and their comments have been much appreciated and strongly responded to. Among them are my pastor, Rev. Tim Vander Haar; our husband-and-wife team of music directors, Tom and Dr. Solie Clark; my brother-in-law, Howard Means, a published writer and free-lance editor, who regularly gives me tough but helpful feed-back; a colleague UCC pastor and writer, and very dear friend of my wife and me, Rev. Janice Springer; my niece, Dr. Carolyn Schott Haury, Organist and Music Director of St. Paul Lutheran Church of Dearborn, Michigan; and various members of the First Presbyterian Men's Breakfast group, especially Ara Demirjian.

But the job of editing I must confess fell most heavily upon my wife, Mary Ellen, who has spent countless hours in

---

Dogmatics, for the English-speaking world. Barth, of course, is well known for his reply to the liberal historical Jesus school of thought in the early 20th century.

reading and re-reading the manuscript and in discussing with me a better way of expressing one thought or another. Besides other wifely graces that will go unmentioned here, she has added one more immense evidence of my great wisdom thirty-four years ago when I married her!

Another dear friend of my wife and me, Kendra Stanley-Mills is a busy free-lance photographer who gave generously of her time to help design and provide an illustration for the cover of this book. I am very grateful for her help.

My publishers and I thank the owners of the copyright of Warner Salman's painting, *Christ at Heart's Door,* Warner Press of Anderson, Indiana, for permission to use that image on the cover of this book. I have vivid memories from my earliest spiritual learnings in Sunday School of the strong impression on me by that popular painting, and I very much welcome its appearance on my book along with images of a modern city in my life today.

Finally, I thank numerous workers with Xlibris Corporation, especially Kim Oliver and Jean Reeves, who have assisted me in the publication of this book, and the artists who designed the cover from my amateurish sketches.